I Can Make

COSTUMES

Makerspace Projects

DISCARD

W9-BJK-253

Emily Reid

WINDMILL BOOKS
New York

Published in 2016 by **Windmill Books**, an Imprint of Rosen Publishing
29 East 21st Street, New York, NY 10010

Copyright © 2016 Windmill Books

All rights reserved. No part of this book may be reproduced in any form
without permission in writing from the publisher, except by a reviewer.

Developed and produced for Rosen by BlueAppleWorks Inc.

Creative Director: Melissa McClellan
Managing Editor for BlueAppleWorks: Melissa McClellan
Designer: T.J. Choleva
Photo Research: Jane Reid
Editor: Marcia Abramson
Craft Artisan: Janet Kompare-Fritz

Photo Credits: Cover center image camilla$$/Shutterstock; cover background image, title page
background Jcomp/Shutterstock; cover insets, title page, TOC, p. 6 bottom, 8–9, 10–11, 12–13, 14–15, 16–17,
18–19, 20–21, 22–23, 24–25, 26–27 Austen Photography; p. 4 left, 5 first row Photka/Dreamstime; p. 4 right
Ermolaevamariya/Dreamstime; p. 4 right bottom Richard Thomas/Dreamstime; p. 5 first row right Ghassan
Safi/Dreamstime; p. 5 second row left Lyudmila Suvorova /Dreamstime; p. 5 second row middle Waldoreyes/
Dreamstime; p. 5 second row right Sergey Mostovoy/Dreamstime; p. 5 third row left Design56/Dreamstime,
Robert Byron/Dreamstime; p. 5 third row middle Rozaliya/Dreamstime; p. 5 third row right (left to right)
Crackerclips/Dreamstime; Les Cunliffe/Dreamstime; Jerryb8/Dreamstime; p. 5 fourth row left Romval/
Dreamstime; p. 5 fourth row right (left to right clockwise) antpkr/Thinkstock; Kelpfish/Dreamstime;Vasiliy
Koval/Dreamstime; Jirk4/Dreamstime; Gradts/Dreamstime; sodapix sodapix/Thinkstock; p. 6 top Jakub
Krechowicz/Dreamstime; p. 6 middle Steveheap/Dreamstime; p. 9 top right Sonja Gehrke/Dreamstime;
p. 11 top right Tose/Dreamstime; p. 13 top right Designwerk/Dreamstime; p. 15 top right Gnsin/Creative
Commons; p. 17 top right Eagleflying/Dreamstime; p. 19 top right Krutenyuk/Dreamstime; p. 21 top right
Nelieta/Dreamstime; p. 23 top right Martin Malchev/Dreamstime; p. 25 top right Sophie Gengembre
Anderson/Public Domain; p. 27 top right Ian Scott/Dreamstime.

Cataloging-in-Publication-Data

Reid, Emily.
I can make costumes / by Emily Reid.
p. cm. — (Makerspace projects)
Includes index.
ISBN 978-1-4777-5635-5 (pbk.)
ISBN 978-1-4777-5634-8 (6 pack)
ISBN 978-1-4777-5558-7 (library binding)
1. Costume — Juvenile literature. 2. Handicraft — Juvenile literature. I. Title.
TT633.R45 2016
646.4'78—d23

Manufactured in the United States of America

CPSIA Compliance Information: Batch #WS15WM: For Further Information contact: Rosen Publishing, New York, New York at 1-800-237-9932

R0447876349

CONTENTS

Materials 4

Techniques 6

Space Alien 8

Lion 10

Pirate 12

Robot 14

Ballerina 16

Zombie 18

Wizard 20

Superhero 22

Fairy 24

Shark 26

Headpiece for Masks 28

Accessories 29

Patterns 30

Glossary 32

For More Information 32

Index 32

MATERIALS

To make great costumes, you need the right materials and a makerspace where you can think and create. Your family may have a permanent makerspace set up for crafting, or you can create one whenever you need it. You may already have many of the supplies shown here. Your family can buy anything else you need at a craft store or dollar store. Organize your supplies in boxes or plastic bins, and you will be ready to create in your makerspace.

A note about patterns

Many of the costumes in this book use patterns or **templates**. Trace the pattern, cut the pattern and then place it on the material you want to cut out. You can either tape it in place and cut both the pattern and material, or trace around the pattern onto the material and then cut it out.

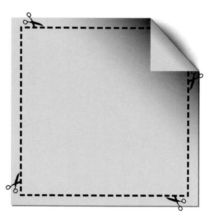

RECYCLABLES

You can make many of the costumes in this book with materials found around the house. Save recyclables (newspapers, cardboard boxes, mailing tubes, cereal boxes, tin cans, and more) to use in your craft projects.
Use your imagination and have fun!

A note about measurements

Measurements are given in U.S. form with metric in brackets. The metric conversion is rounded to make it easier to measure.

PAINT AND MARKERS

TISSUE PAPER

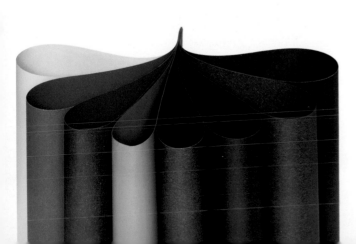

CRAFT FOAM SHEETS

FELT

GLITTER

CRAFT GEMS

GLUE AND TAPE

PAPER

TOOLS

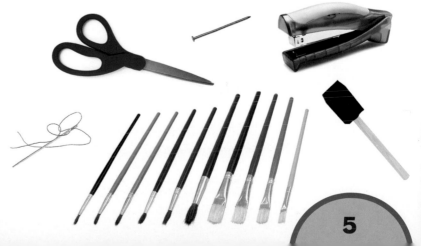

TECHNIQUES

Have fun while making your costumes! Be creative. Your project does not have to look just like the one in this book. If you don't have a certain material, think of something similar you could use.

The following techniques will help you create your costumes.

Using your creativity to make crafts is a very rewarding activity. When you are finished, you can say with great pride, **"I made that!"**

THREADING A NEEDLE

Threading a needle can be frustrating. The following tips will help.

- Cut more thread than you think you will need.
- Wet one end of the thread in your mouth.
- Poke it through the needle opening.
- Pull some of the thread through until you have an even amount and make a double knot.
- If you are using thicker thread like embroidery thread, do not double up the thread. Just pull a small amount through and make the knot at the other end.

EASIEST METHOD

- Use a metal needle threader.
- Push the metal threader through the needle hole, put the thread through the loop, and then pull the needle threader back through the needle.

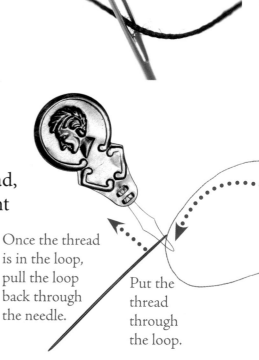

Once the thread is in the loop, pull the loop back through the needle.

Put the thread through the loop.

SEWING FABRIC

The whipstitch works great with felt. It is used to sew two pieces together.

- Place the needle and knotted thread in between the two pieces of felt and up through the top layer of felt.
- Take the needle behind both layers of felt at point 1.
- Pull the needle through both layers of felt at point 2.
- Continue stitching until finished.

LARK'S HEAD KNOT

The lark's head knot, or cow hitch, is easy to make. Hitch knots are used to connect one thing to another.

- Find the halfway point in your cord or rope and fold in half there.
- Put the fold over whatever you are tying the cord or rope to, such as a **dowel** or post. The loop should have a U shape with both ends coming over the dowel toward the front.
- Pass both ends of the cord or rope through the loop from back to front.
- Pull on both lines to tighten the knot.

MAKING HOLES IN CARDBOARD

Some projects require holes to be made in cardboard. There are several methods.

- Use the tip of a pair of sharp scissors to create the hole. Push the tip of the scissors through the hole and then turn the scissors. If you use this method, always point the scissors away from yourself!

- Small holes — push a nail through the cardboard. Always point the nail away from yourself!

- Medium holes — start with the nail to make a small hole, then push a Phillips screwdriver through the small hole to make it larger.

- Big holes — start with the nail to make a small hole, then push a Phillips screwdriver through the small hole to make it larger. Then insert your scissors and cut the hole to the size you want.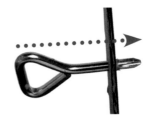

BE PREPARED
- Read through the instructions and make sure you have all the materials you need.
- Cover your work area with newspaper or cardboard.
- Clean up your makerspace when you are finished making your project.

BE SAFE
- Ask for help when you need it.
- Ask for permission to use tools.
- Be careful when using knives, scissors, and sewing needles.

SPACE ALIEN

No one knows if there are space aliens or what they might look like. So there are no rules for making an alien costume. Just use your imagination!

You'll Need

- Foam craft sheets, 12 x 18 inches (30 x 45 cm)
  - 4 sheets of green
  - 2 sheets of blue
  - 1 sheet of white
  - 1 sheet of black
  - 1 sheet of purple
- Paper for tracing
- Pencil
- Scissors
- Glue
- Thin craft wire
- Tape
- Paper cups (2)
- Green tissue paper
- Foam balls (5)
- Googly eyes (3 large, 2 small)
- Pipe cleaners (3)

Cut

Tape wire to back of ear.

Cover cup in green tissue paper.

1 Trace and cut out the patterns on page 31. Use the rectangle pattern to cut a piece of green foam. Cut out the smaller rectangle opening in the center. Now cut out the semicircle piece. Glue the large rectangle to the bottom of the straight edge of the semicircle.

2 Use the pattern to cut two ears from green foam. Glue these to the back of the semicircle, on the sides. Cut a piece of craft wire that is 12 inches (30 cm) long, and bend it into a U shape. Tape it to the back of your ears. Cut two more ears, a bit smaller than your first, and glue them over the wire.

3 Cut the bottom half off two paper cups. Glue green tissue paper to the cups. Cover all the foam balls with glue and tissue paper. Glue the two large googly eyes onto two of the foam balls, place in the cups, and glue to each ear.

Glue the three layers together.

Did You Know?

Science fiction has been depicting aliens with big eyes and gray skin since at least 1893.

4 Using the patterns, cut out the center eye from blue, white, and black foam. Glue the black circle to the white circle and white circle to the blue eye. Glue the eye to the semicircle green piece.

Glue circles on mask.

5 Cut out 14 small circles from the leftover green foam and 11 from the purple foam. Glue them all over the mask.

6 Stick craft wire, about 6 inches (15 cm) in length, halfway into the other three foam balls, then wrap pipe cleaners around this. Tape them to the back of the mask. See page 28 for making a headband.

Tip

Stick the pipe cleaner into the ball where the wire is and add a bit of glue to secure it.

LION

Act like the king of the jungle with this lion mask. Roar! To look even more like a lion, wear lion-colored clothes and make a tail out of leftover felt.

You'll Need

- ✔ Paper plates (3 or 4)
- ✔ Pen or pencil
- ✔ Scissors
- ✔ Brush
- ✔ Glue
- ✔ Yellow tissue paper
- ✔ Light brown, black, and dark brown felt
- ✔ Toilet paper roll
- ✔ Pipe cleaners (3)
- ✔ White foam sheet
- ✔ Cardboard
- ✔ Colored paper (orange)
- ✔ Tape (optional)

Draw and cut out eyes and mouth.

Trim

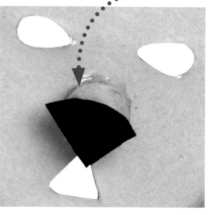

Glue

1 Draw eyes and mouth on a paper plate (if thin, glue two paper plates together). Cut these pieces out. Using a brush, cover the whole paper plate with glue and then yellow tissue paper. Remove tissue paper from the eye holes. Brush glue over the tissue paper. Leave to dry.

2 Using another paper plate, cut out two rounded ovals with bottom sliced off. These will be your ears. Cover these with glue and tissue paper. Cut out U-shapes from light brown felt and glue on top of ears. Glue ears into place, slightly on top and to the side of head.

3 Cut off 1 inch (2.5 cm) of the toilet paper roll and glue it above the mouth. Stuff inside with tissue paper. Cover with glue and yellow tissue paper. Cut a rounded triangle piece of black felt and glue halfway down the nose.

Trim

Glue

Did You Know?

Male lions have a fancy mane around their neck, and they are bigger than the females. Lionesses, though, are better hunters.

4 Using 3 inches (8 cm) of the toilet paper roll, cut it in half. This will be the snout. Glue light brown felt over this and then trim the felt to the roll. Glue it to the plate on an angle on the left and right side of nose pointing down.

5 Cut out three eyes from pattern on page 31 from black, light brown, and darker brown felt. Cut out holes for eyes. Glue them over the eye hole on paper plate, largest first and then the two smaller ones.

Glue strips to plate.

6 Cut the pipe cleaners in thirds and glue to snout, having three whiskers **protruding** on each side. Cut white teeth triangles from white foam and glue below the snout.

Glue

7 Cut out 36 two-inch-wide (5 cm) strips of cardboard. Cut half 24 inches (61 cm) long and half 20 inches (51 cm) long. Rip strips of colored paper, downward, creating a tear and a curl. Glue one end of the torn strip to one end of a cardboard strip. Glue or tape the cardboard strips around the back of the plate. Optional: Glue a paper plate over top to give additional strength. Cut out the eyes and mouth.

8 Using the light brown felt, cut out 6-inch x 1½-inch (15 cm x 4 cm) strips and using scissors, cut a fringe. Glue these strips around the outside rim of plate, covering up the strips of construction paper and cardboard. See page 28 for making a headband.

PIRATE

Become the greatest pirate of the high seas with this costume. Rule the waves while collecting treasure wherever you go.

You'll Need

- ✔ Paper for tracing
- ✔ Pen or pencil
- ✔ Cardboard (2 pieces)
- ✔ Scissors
- ✔ Glue
- ✔ Felt (black, red, and white)
- ✔ Tape
- ✔ Hairband (thin black)

Glue   Trim   Fold and glue.

1 Trace the pattern on page 30 and cut it out. Place this on cardboard and cut two pieces. Cover both pieces of cardboard with glue. Place two pieces of black felt over the cardboard and smooth out the felt. When dry cut the felt to the edges of the cardboard.

2 Cut two pieces of red felt, as above. One piece should be about twice as long as the hat piece. The other piece should be a bit shorter than the long piece.

3 Glue the long piece to the inside of the front hat piece, slightly slanted so that it looks like a scarf coming down. At the edge of hat, fold over the red piece and glue down. Glue the second shorter piece of red felt to the corner and do the same fold over.

Glue ·········→

 Use strong glue to glue the two ends of your hat together, along the ends with the top corners. Make sure there are at least 2 inches (5 cm) glued together.

4 Use strong glue to glue the two ends of your hat together, along the ends with the top corners. Make sure there are at least 2 inches (5 cm) glued together.

Glue trim on
the top edge.

Did You Know?

Pirates flew a flag known as the Jolly Roger when they were about to attack a ship. They used the image of a skull and crossbones to frighten people.

5 Using the pattern piece on page 30, cut skull and crossbones from white felt. Cut out 1-inch (3 cm) strips of white felt, which will cover the top edge of the hat as trim. Glue on the skull and bones. Glue on the white trim.

Pirate's Eye Patch

Cut cardboard into a square that will cover your eye area. Round the edges to make almost a heart shape. Cover with glue and glue black felt over to cover front, wrapping over to the back side. Before you cover the back, tape down the two ends of your black hairband. Then cover the back with second piece of felt that will hide the edges and hairband. Put on and ahoy matey!

Hairband

See page 29 for the spyglass instructions.

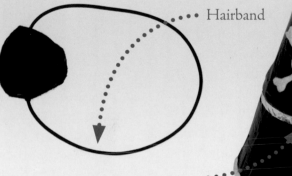

ROBOT

When you are wearing this costume, remember to walk, talk, and act like a robot.

You'll Need

- 12-inch (30 cm) dowels (2)
- Foam balls (3)
- Glue
- Brush
- Tinfoil
- Paper towel rolls (4)
- Tissue paper
- Tape
- Big plastic bowl or garden pot
- Scissors
- Cardboard
- Small paper or foam cup
- Buttons (optional)
- Cardboard box for body (optional)

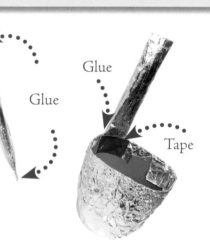

Leave extra tinfoil at the bottom.

Glue

Glue

Tape

Tape

1 Poke one dowel through two of the foam balls, leaving space between them. Poke another dowel halfway through one foam ball, keeping it at the top of the dowel. Brush glue over both the dowels and foam balls and then wrap both in tinfoil (this helps the foil stick better).

2 Brush glue on four paper towel rolls and wrap with tinfoil. Stuff them with tissue paper. Press each end flat and glue together. Cover the outside of the bowl with glue and then tinfoil. Tape each of the covered rolls, flat side down, on the inside of the bowl. Put some glue on the other side of the roll and press to the bowl. Space them out evenly.

3 Cut a strip of cardboard about 4 inches (10 cm) wide and 2 inches (5 cm) longer than the bowl or pot. You may have to cut two pieces and tape them together. Cover with glue and tinfoil. Tape the ends together. Tape the bottoms of the four paper rolls to this circle.

Glue headpiece to base.

Glue

Did You Know?

The ASIMO robot can run like a human and even kick a soccer ball. ASIMO tours the world to show how its maker, the Honda Motor Company, is learning to improve robots.

4 Cut a hole large enough for your head to fit through on a 9-inch x 14-inch (23 cm x 36 cm) piece of cardboard. Cover it with glue and tinfoil. Glue or tape it to the headpiece. Cut some circles and rectangle shapes out of cardboard and cover with glue and tinfoil. Cover a small paper or foam cup with glue and tinfoil. Glue or tape the shapes, cup, and dowels to the headpiece.

Cut holes for arms and head.

Robot's Body

1 Find a box big enough for your body to fit into, cut out a hole at the top big enough for your head to fit through, and holes for your arms to fit through on either side. Cover with tinfoil. Add extra pieces of cardboard that are covered in tinfoil, for extra buttons or speakers or shapes.

2 Optional: Add a bottom piece by taping additional strips covered in tinfoil to the box. Cover a strip of cardboard long enough to go around the front of the box in glue and tinfoil. Glue or tape it to the box.

Tip

Using markers, you can draw on the robot as well.

BALLERINA

Do you dream of doing pirouettes on a grand stage? Make this ballerina costume and dance like no one is watching.

You'll Need

- ✔ Elastic band 1 inch (2.5 cm) wide and 24 inches (61 cm) long
- ✔ Needle and thread
- ✔ Scissors
- ✔ Fabric
- ✔ Paper for tracing
- ✔ Pen or pencil
- ✔ Cardboard
- ✔ Glue
- ✔ Brush
- ✔ Yellow tissue paper
- ✔ Glitter
- ✔ Jewels
- ✔ Elastic band 1 inch (2.5 cm) wide and 7 inches (18 cm) long
- ✔ Tape or stapler

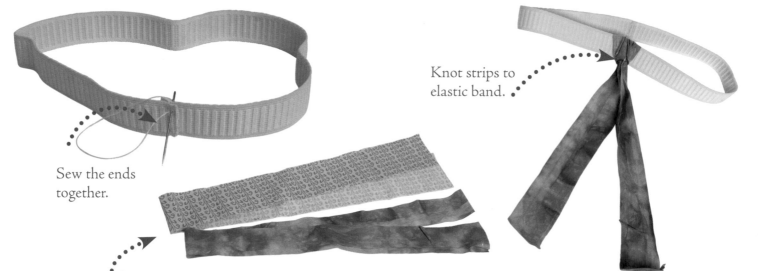

Sew the ends together.

Cut strips. The width does not need to be exact.

Knot strips to elastic band.

1 Sew the ends of the longer elastic together with a firm tight stitch. This needs to be strong as this is going to hold everything up and together.

2 Cut fabric strips about 2 inches x 27 inches (5 cm x 70 cm) in length. Cut about 50 strips of material. If the fabric is thin enough, double it and cut two strips at a time.

3 Fold a fabric strip in half and tie it to the elastic loop using the lark's head knot (shown on page 7). Repeat until all the strips are attached to the elastic loop.

Cut crown and
shapes from
cardboard.

Did You Know?

The toe of a ballerina's
pointe shoe holds a
box made of layers
of fabric or paper
hardened by glue.
The dancer uses the
box for balance.

Ballerina's Crown

1 Trace and cut out the crown pattern on page 30. Use
the pattern to cut a crown shape from thin cardboard.
Cut out diamond and circle shapes from cardboard. Glue the
cardboard diamonds and circles to your crown.

Cover with glue and
yellow tissue paper.

2 Brush glue over the crown and lay a
piece of yellow tissue paper over it.
Smooth the tissue paper down and wrap it
around the edges of the cardboard. While
this glue is still wet, sprinkle glitter over the
entire surface, including the sides.

Glue on jewels.

Attach elastic band.

3 Once this has
dried, glue the
jewels on your crown,
especially the areas you
have raised with the
cardboard shapes.

4 Staple or tape at least
1 inch (2.5 cm) of
each end of the shorter elastic
band to each end of your
crown.

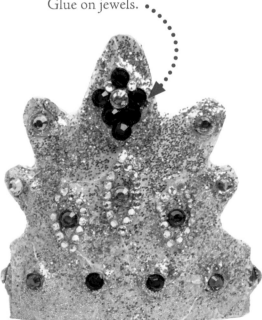

ZOMBIE

Zombies are fictional undead creatures, usually depicted as mindless, **reanimated** human corpses. Wear this mask and join the undead.

You'll Need

- ✔ Foam craft sheets (gray, light brown, dark brown, yellow)
- ✔ Pen or pencil
- ✔ Scissors
- ✔ Duct tape
- ✔ Glue
- ✔ Markers
- ✔ Pipe cleaner
- ✔ Foam ball
- ✔ Googly eye
- ✔ Cheap wig (from dollar store)
- ✔ Sponge
- ✔ Red paint and brush

Tape small piece to the large piece.

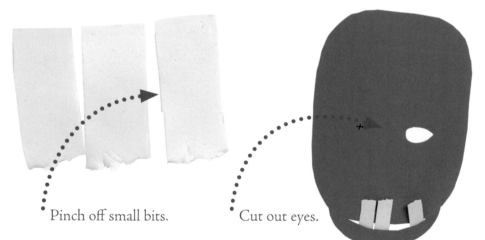

Pinch off small bits.

Cut out eyes.

1 Draw your zombie head on a gray foam sheet, using most of the sheet. From another gray sheet cut out the bottom of the mouth, curved and long enough to almost cover the base of the main head. Tape this piece to the bottom of the head.

2 Cut out three teeth from the yellow craft foam sheet. Make the edges ragged by ripping small pieces from them. Glue or tape these to the bottom lip.

3 Place the headpiece against your face. Use a marker to make a mark on the foam where your eyes are. Take the foam away from your face and cut out holes for eyes.

Cut eyebrows and under-eye shadows out of brown foam.

Did You Know?

People dress up as zombies to play games, raise money for charity, or just have fun. Thousands attend zombie walks held worldwide.

4 Using the extra pieces of gray craft foam and two different color brown sheets, cut out semicircles and circles that you can glue to outline your eyes.

Stick pipe cleaner into foam ball.

5 Make a small slit for your nose. Roll some leftover gray craft foam in a cone shape. Stuff the cone with more gray scraps and some red felt scraps. Make slits on other parts of face and do the same thing, **representing** cuts and peeling of skin. Gross!

6 Cut a small piece of pipe cleaner and push it into the foam ball and glue it in place. Use a red marker to make the blood veins in eye. Glue the googly eye to center. Bend the other end of the pipe cleaner. Put it through one eye on the mask. Tape the end to the back of mask.

Paint sponge red.

7 Glue the wig to the top of the mask at the back and drape it over the mask. Cut holes into a small piece of sponge and paint it red. When it is dry, glue it near the top forehead, moving hair out of the way and then gluing some of the hair down on top. This represents exposed brain. Yuck!

8 Attach the mask to a headpiece, see page 28.

WIZARD

Make magic happen when you make this wizard hat and wand. You could even add a long white beard made of cotton.

You'll Need

- ✔ Poster board
- ✔ Ruler
- ✔ Tape
- ✔ Scissors
- ✔ Thin craft wire
- ✔ Glue
- ✔ Double-sided tape
- ✔ 2 colors of felt (1 large piece of felt that will cover your hat and smaller piece of felt for decorating hat)

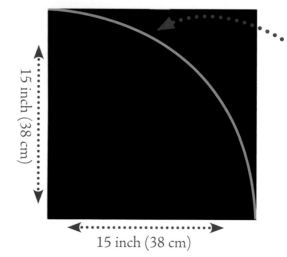

15 inch (38 cm)

15 inch (38 cm)

Trim

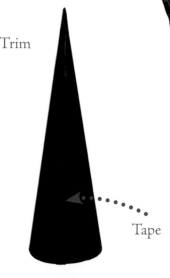

Tape

Tape each row as you twist it around the cone.

1 Cut a piece of the long end of the poster board so that it is square. Cut a 15-inch (38 cm) quarter circle by cutting from corner to corner as shown above.

2 Bring the two ends of the quarter circle together and join base and top with tape, to form a cone. Adjust the cone so that the base fits your head. Once you find the right size, tape the whole seam to hold in place.

3 Optional step: This will give the hat strength and make it bendable. Push the wire into the top of the hat and tape down. Slowly wind the wire around the hat leaving around 3-inch (8 cm) spacing. Tape the wire into place.

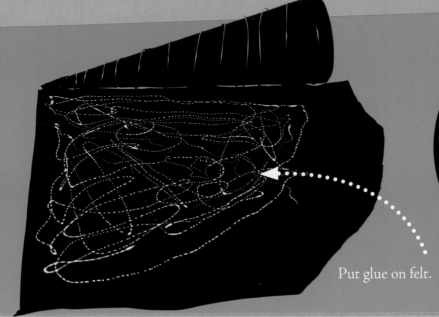

Put glue on felt.

Did You Know?

Wizards from ancient Merlin to Gandalf to Dumbledore have been depicted with long white beards. This tradition may have started with Norse legends.

4 Cut out a semicircle of felt at least 2 inches (5 cm) bigger than your hat. Use tape to hold one side in place. Cover the felt with glue. Use a piece of double-sided tape to hold the other edge to the felt after pulling the felt around the hat base. It is okay if it is not perfectly smooth as this gives it texture. (If you did step 3, when the glue dries, squish the hat down and bend it a bit, pushing from the top.)

Cut out felt shapes.

5 Cut out stars, crescent moons or other shapes (you can draw them or use the pattern on page 31) from the other color of felt and glue them onto the hat.

6 For the base of the wizard hat, roll up the base edges of the hat to make a brim. Use double-sided tape to hold them in place.

Tip To make the hat taller or shorter, change the size of the quarter circle.

See page 29 for the magic wand instructions.

SUPERHERO

Prepare to fight crime and evil with this superhero costume. Role-play and come up with which superhuman powers you have. Enjoy saving the day!

You'll Need

- ✔ Polyester tablecloth (rectangular)
- ✔ Ruler
- ✔ Chalk
- ✔ Scissors
- ✔ Glue
- ✔ Felt
- ✔ Button
- ✔ Needle and thread (same color as cape)
- ✔ Paper for tracing
- ✔ Pen or pencil
- ✔ Toilet paper rolls (2)

Cut corner off.

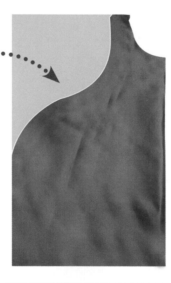

Cut

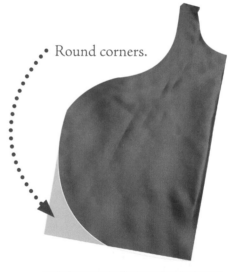

Round corners.

1 Fold the tablecloth in half lengthwise. With the fold on your right, measure 7 inches (18 cm) down from the top and 5 inches (13 cm) from the fold. Make marks with chalk. Connect the two marks with a semicircle. Cut along the chalk line.

2 Make another mark 3 inches (8 cm) to the left of the last cut. Measure 18 inches (46 cm) from the bottom and make a mark. Join these two marks as shown above. Cut along the chalk line.

3 Open up the cape, and wrap it around your neck to see if it is big enough and you will be able to tie the ends. If not, cut the collar larger. Cut the bottom of your cape, making rounded edges.

Sew felt and button to collar.

Did You Know?

Legends have told of beings with super powers for thousands of years, but the first modern superhero was Superman in the 1930s.

4 On one side of your collar tab, glue on a circular piece of felt that is a bit bigger than your button. Sew your button on top of this. On the opposite tab of your collar make a slit that will allow your button to go through.

Superhero Wrist Bands

Tape the inside edges.

Cut down middle of tube.

Cut one side of each toilet paper roll. Cut a piece of leftover tablecloth that will cover each roll with a bit going on the inside of the roll. Glue this to the toilet paper roll. Cut out shapes from the felt and glue on top of the wristbands.

Tip

It might help to gently hold the toilet paper roll and fabric in place with an elastic band until it dries, to keep the shape firm.

Superhero Mask

Trace and cut out the pattern on page 31 and place over a folded piece of leftover tablecloth. Cut out the material. Cut out the eye holes. Using small pieces of felt, decorate your mask on either side of the eyes.

Decorate with felt.

FAIRY

Become a magical fairy with these dreamy wings. Create a story to go with your costume.

You'll Need

- ✔ Cardboard (2 large pieces)
- ✔ Paper for tracing
- ✔ Pen or pencil
- ✔ Scissors
- ✔ Paint and paintbrush
- ✔ Glitter glue
- ✔ Gems
- ✔ Cellophane paper
- ✔ Tape
- ✔ Glue
- ✔ Elastic band 1/2 inch (1.3 cm) wide

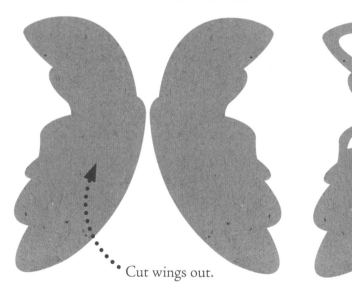

Cut wings out.

Cut shapes out of cardboard wings.

1 Trace the pattern for the wings from page 30 onto a piece of paper. Using the pattern as a guide, cut two wings from a piece of cardboard. Flip the pattern over and cut two more wings from the second piece of cardboard.

2 Cut the shapes out of the pattern and tape to the first wing. Use the shapes as a guide to cut the shapes from the cardboard. Start each cut by poking a hole in the cardboard. Flip the shapes over and cut them from the other wings.

3 Paint the outsides of the wings with white paint. Once dry, decorate painted wings with glitter glue, gems, and other paint colors. Let dry.

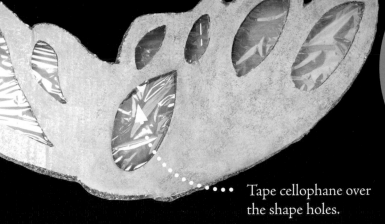

Tape cellophane over the shape holes.

Did You Know?

The idea of fairies comes from European folklore, especially from the British Isles, in pre-Christian times.

4 When dry, turn the wings painted side down. Cut cellophane to cover the holes in wings for one left wing and then for one right wing. Tape or glue it down. Glue the matching wings together.

5 Place wings decorated side down and space them side by side. Cut a piece of cardboard into a rectangle sized to 3 inches x 8 inches (8 cm x 20 cm). Paint both sides white but only decorate one side. Glue or tape this piece about halfway down, taping at least 2 inches (5 cm) of the ends of each wing.

Glue wings together.

Tape

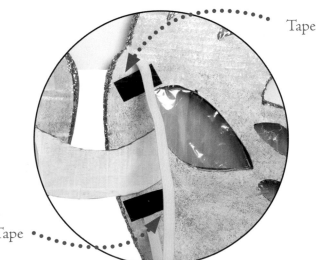

Tape

6 Cut two pieces of elastic 12 inches (30 cm) in length. Glue or tape at least 1 inch (2.5 cm) of each of the same side ends of the elastics to the wings. Adjust the length until the wings fit tightly.

Another Idea!

You can make this without the cutouts by cutting only a right and left wing and skipping steps 2 and 4.

SHARK

Tell everyone to watch out for the shark attack when you make and wear this costume!

You'll Need

✔ Gray knit hat (from dollar store)
✔ Chalk
✔ Foam craft sheets (white, gray, black)
✔ Scissors
✔ Glue
✔ Felt (red and black)
✔ Paper for tracing
✔ Pen or pencil
✔ White paint
✔ Tissue paper

Cut •••••

Cut triangles of white foam.

Glue red felt. •••••

1 Put the hat over a friend's head and with white chalk, draw a circle over the front where your face will be exposed. Remove the hat from their head and cut this circle out.

2 Cut a 1½-inch (4 cm) strip of white foam sheet. Make **diagonal** cuts to make triangles for shark's teeth. Glue them onto the inside of the hole in the hat.

3 Cut out a long thin strip of red felt with a slight curve. Glue to the inside of the hole with some of the top and bottom showing behind the teeth.

Make two eyes.

Did You Know?

Sharks grow teeth quickly to replace broken or lost ones. They may use 20,000 teeth in a lifetime.

4 Cut out two ovals of white foam for the shark's eyes, then two circles of the black foam for the pupils of the shark's eyes. Glue the pupil to each eye and then glue whole eye to each side of the hat.

5 Trace a shark fin pattern from page 30 and cut out two pieces of white foam. Paint the fins gray. Glue both sides together leaving the bottom base open. Cut the tabs indicated on the pattern. Once dried, stuff the fin with tissue paper.

Glue the fin to the hat.

6 Turn hat over to the back side of the shark's head and carefully cut a slit through the first layer of hat, around 5½ inches (14 cm) in length. Glue the shark fin, base tabs entering the slit, to the inside of the hat which is the back of the head. Now go get 'em, sharks!

Tip
Put a head-sized ball inside the hat while you are working on this mask.

27

HEADPIECE FOR MASKS

This headpiece will work for all three masks in this book.

You'll Need
- ✔ Paper for tracing
- ✔ Pen or pencil
- ✔ Scissors
- ✔ Poster board

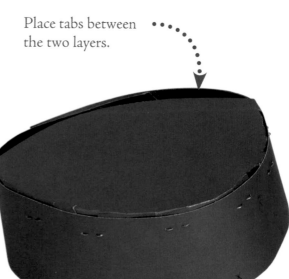

Place tabs between the two layers.

Staple the two ends together.

1 Use the pattern on page 31 to draw and cut out larger versions of the shapes in the image above. Use these larger patterns to trace and cut out pieces on poster board.

2 Put one end of the folded headband inside the fold of the other end. Check to see if it fits around your head. Staple the two ends together.

3 Cut tabs on cap top and bend them down. Center the cap in the middle of the headpiece and insert the tabs in between the folds. Staple in place. Center the mask on the cap. Glue or tape the mask to the cap.

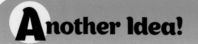 **Another Idea!** If you have an old baseball cap, you can cut the brim off, and use that as the headpiece.

ACCESSORIES
WIZARD MAGIC WAND

You will need:
- ✔ Stick
- ✔ Yarn
- ✔ Glue
- ✔ Tissue paper
- ✔ Glitter
- ✔ Marble

Wrap yarn.

Glue a marble.

1 Wind a piece of yarn around a stick, spacing it out. Glue each end of the yarn or string to the stick.

2 Cover the stick and yarn with glue and wrap tissue paper over it.

3 Brush glue over the tissue paper. Sprinkle with glitter. Glue a marble to the top of the stick to make a wizard wand.

PIRATE SPYGLASS

You will need:
- ✔ Large paper or plastic cup
- ✔ Small paper or foam cup
- ✔ Scissors
- ✔ Tape
- ✔ Toilet paper roll
- ✔ Black duct tape
- ✔ Tinfoil
- ✔ White felt
- ✔ Glue

Tape

1 Cut a hole in the base of both the large cup and the small cup. Place the small cup on the larger cup and tape them together.

2 If necessary, cut a paper roll up one side and fold to make a smaller roll that will fit into the hole in the paper cup. Tape the roll up the side and put the roll into the paper cup hole and tape it in place.

3 Cover the entire piece with black duct tape. Cut strips of tinfoil and glue them to each seam of the cups. At the neck of the toilet paper roll, make a wide piece of tinfoil to cover the top.

4 Take another piece of tinfoil and fold it a few times over, making a thick but small band, to place just down from the top of toilet paper roll. Cut skull and crossbones from white felt. Glue this to the middle portion of spyglass.

PATTERNS

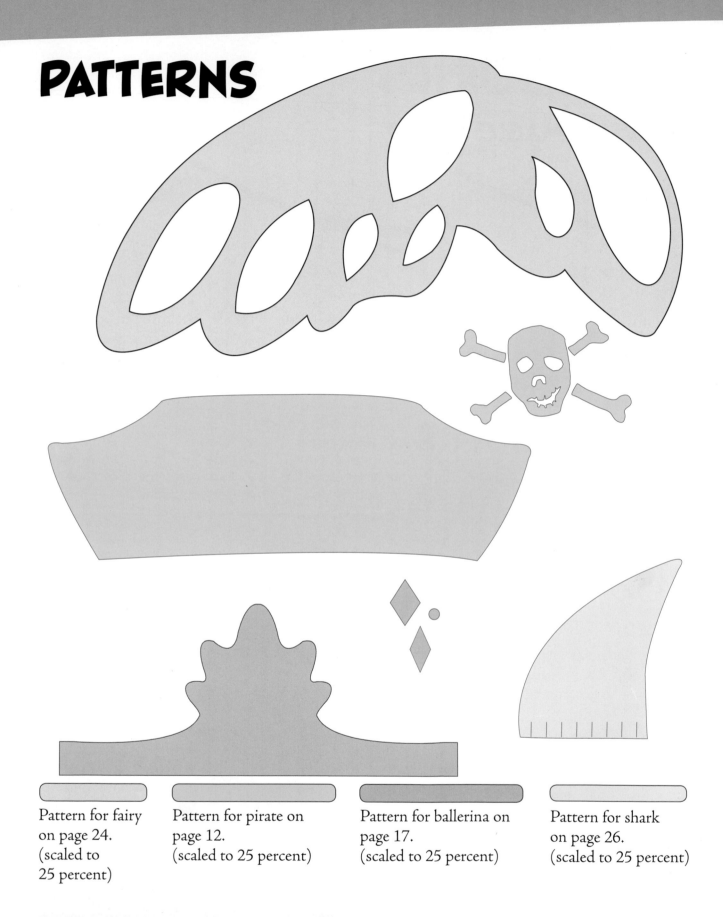

Pattern for fairy on page 24. (scaled to 25 percent)

Pattern for pirate on page 12. (scaled to 25 percent)

Pattern for ballerina on page 17. (scaled to 25 percent)

Pattern for shark on page 26. (scaled to 25 percent)

Note: Templates on pages 30-31 are scaled to 25 or 50 percent of the original size. Use a scanner or a printer to resize the templates. (400% or 200%)

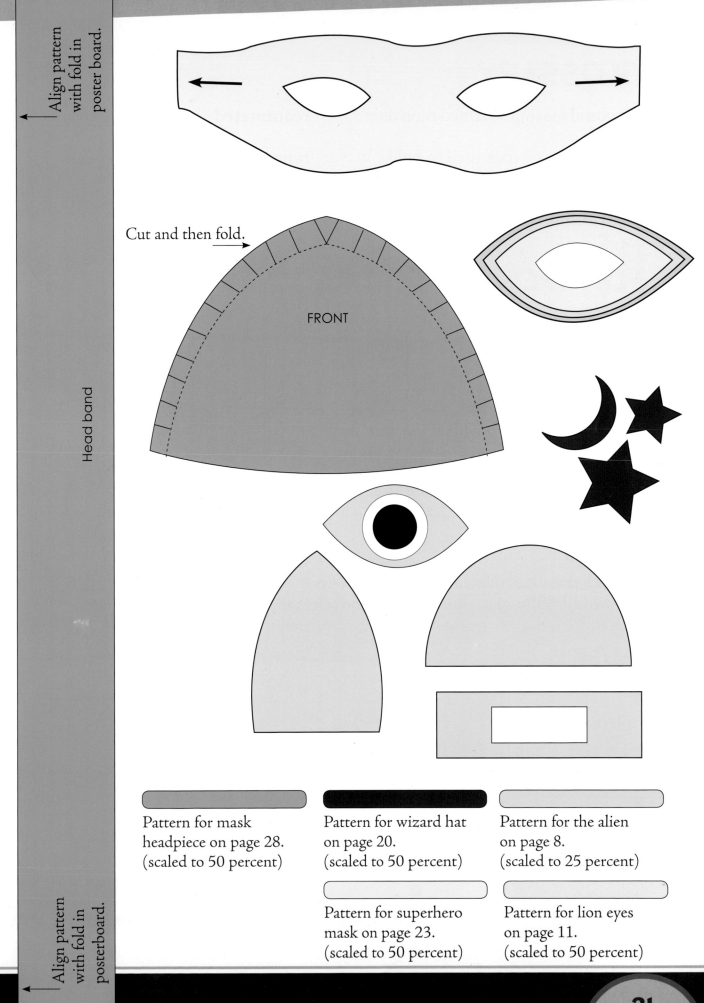

Align pattern with fold in poster board.

Head band

Align pattern with fold in posterboard.

Cut and then fold.

FRONT

Pattern for mask
headpiece on page 28.
(scaled to 50 percent)

Pattern for wizard hat
on page 20.
(scaled to 50 percent)

Pattern for the alien
on page 8.
(scaled to 25 percent)

Pattern for superhero
mask on page 23.
(scaled to 50 percent)

Pattern for lion eyes
on page 11.
(scaled to 50 percent)

GLOSSARY

diagonal Having a slanted direction.

dowel A peg or stick used to hold pieces together.

protruding Sticking out.

reanimated Having been given new life.

represent To be an example of.

template A shape used as a pattern.

FOR MORE INFORMATION

FURTHER READING

Carlson, Alyn. *The Paper Hat Book.*
Beverly MA: Quarry Books, 2014.

Henry, Sally, and Trevor Cook. *Making Masks.*
New York, NY: PowerKids Press, 2011.

Reeder, Dan. *Papier-Mâché Monsters: Turn Trinkets and Trash into Magnificent Monstrosities.*
Layton, UT: Gibbs Smith, 2009.

WEBSITES

For web resources related to the subject of this book, go to:
www.windmillbooks.com/weblinks and select this book's title.

INDEX

B
ballerina 16, 17
F
fairy 24, 25
H
headpiece 28
L
lark's head knot 7
lion 10, 11

M
magic wand 21, 29
measurements 4
P
pattern(s) 4, 8, 9, 11, 12, 13, 17, 21, 23, 24, 27, 28, 30, 31
pirate 12, 13, 29
R
recyclables 4
robot 14, 15

S
sewing 6
shark 26, 27
space alien 8, 9
spyglass 29
superhero 22, 23
W
wizard 20, 21, 29
Z
zombie 18, 19